THIS LITTLE
EXPLORER
A PIONEER PRIMER

ISBN 978-1-338-32544-7

12 11 10 9 8 7 6 5 4 3 2 1   18 19 20 21 22 23

Printed in the U.S.A.   40

First Scholastic printing, September 2018

Designed by Laura Roode

THIS LITTLE

EXPLORER

A PIONEER PRIMER

JOAN HOLUB · DANIEL ROODE

SCHOLASTIC INC.

Sailing, flying, excitement galore!

Going where no one has gone before.

Little explorers have great big adventures.

LEIF ERIKSON

This little explorer
was a Viking, big and strong.
He sailed to North America
but did not stay for long.

Leif Erikson was nicknamed "Leif the Lucky."
He was the first European to land in America.

MARCO POLO

This little explorer
went to China with his dad.
Then he wrote a book
about adventures that he had.

Marco Polo was just a teenager when he left for China. He rode camels, saw wild animals, and met a rich emperor.

CHRISTOPHER
COLUMBUS

This little explorer
sailed in 1492.

He was hunting for gold,
and other riches, too.

Christopher Columbus sailed from Spain in ships named the Nina, the Pinta, and the Santa Maria. He hoped to land in Asia but bumped into America instead.

FERDINAND
MAGELLAN

This little explorer
proved the world was round
when others believed
it was only flat ground.

Ferdinand Magellan's ship was the
first to sail around the world.

SACAJAWEA

This little explorer
did her very best
to lead Lewis and Clark
through the American West.

Sacajawea was the Native American guide
for explorers Meriwether Lewis and William Clark.

MATTHEW HENSON

This little explorer
was brave and bold.
He searched for the North Pole,
which was freezing cold.

Matthew Henson and his friend Robert Peary spent many years exploring the icy Arctic at the top of the world.

AMELIA EARHART

This little explorer
showed what women could do.
She did flying tricks
and broke speed records, too.

Amelia Earhart was a famous pilot. She was the first
woman to fly an airplane alone across the Atlantic Ocean.

JACQUES COUSTEAU

This little explorer
dove deep undersea
to study life he found there
and film it for TV.

Jacques Cousteau showed fantastic ocean plants and animals in hopes people would protect them.

EDMUND HILLARY

This little explorer
was a climbing pro.
He hiked up mountains
through ice and snow.

Edmund Hillary was the first to climb to the top of Mount Everest, the highest mountain in the world.

NEIL ARMSTRONG

This little explorer
was an astronaut.
He walked on the moon
and put a flag on the spot.

Neil Armstrong said walking on the moon was, "One small step for man, one giant leap for mankind."

Oceans, mountains, or stars far away,

ZHENG HE

This navy admiral helped China trade with other countries.

AMERIGO VESPUCCI

America was named after this ship navigator.

PONCE DE LEON

On a quest for gold, this sea captain named the state of Florida.

IDA PFEIFFER

One of the first women explorers, she went to the Egyptian pyramids and other lands.

ISABELLA BIRD

This daring author climbed an active volcano and explored the world.

GERTRUDE BELL

This archaeologist worked in the Middle East to protect art and statue

where would you like to explore someday?

First woman to ride a bicycle
around the world.

First person to reach the
South Pole in 1911.

First astronaut to go
into outer space in 1961.

First American woman in outer
space on the space shuttle Challenger.

rst African American woman in outer
pace on the space shuttle Endeavour.